How to Win at Performance Management

Also by Mack Munro

BossTalk: What Every Boss Needs to Know to About Giving Great Presentations

How to Build Better Bosses

How to Be a Great Boss

The New Rules of Engagement: How to Keep Your Superstars Loyal to You

How to Win at Performance Management

By
Mack Munro

First Edition

Main Line Press . Vanleer, TN

How to Win at Performance Management

Printed in the United States of America

ISBN: 978-0-9895795-7-5

Cover Layout
By
Michael Cartwright
CartwrightDesign@att.net

Quantity discounts are available on bulk purchases of this book for
educational training purposes, fund-raising, or gift giving. For more
information, contact us at the address below. Special books, booklets, or book
excerpts can also be created to fit your specific needs. For more information,
contact Marketing Department, Main Line Press,
P.O. Box 75, Vanleer, TN 37181.

Table of Contents

Preface

No single management act can strike fear, apathy, lethargy, or cynical laughter into the hearts of employees than performance management. Call it what you want, an evaluation, annual review, or FITREP, it's all the same. The one act that should turn poor managers and employees into great ones typically causes chaos and low motivation.

Why is this so?

Because performance evaluation can be subjective, it's often up to a manager's perception what good and poor performance look like, and since often a pay raise or bonus is tied to it, employees fear it.

But what if I told you that performance management is the key to management success? It actually is! You'll learn why in this book, but for now, let's have a little fun. I'll let you in on the *Top 10 Ways to Screw Up Performance Management.* See how many of these your company is doing. The good news is, that even if it does all 10, you can make a difference by simply applying the formula and techniques in this book.

Here we go!

#10: Jumping on the "Ditch the Annual Evaluation" Bandwagon

CEOs and sometimes even HR professionals get caught up in the latest fads. Right now there seems to be a general cry to ditch the annual evaluation altogether. While it might make sense in an organization where there has been bias and subjectivity or simply a lot of neglect, you NEED to evaluate performance. Don't ditch it, fix it!

#9: Allowing Managers to Dodge Their Responsibilities

The number one job a manager has is to manage performance. Think about it. If a manager was to spend time giving feedback and coaching performance, it would lead to the employees being more successful. If that happened, then we'd know the job was getting done. The manager could THEN spend time going to meetings, etc.

Managers who don't take the time to coach and guide employee performance are shirking their responsibility! Don't let them get away with it!

#8: Allowing Employees to Dodge Doing Self-Assessments

Self-assessments are the responsibility of the employee. Yes, I know they'll say it's the manager's job to observe and know what the employee is doing, but they can't see everything.

Employees already know how to hide poor performance from their boss but do you want the boss to miss out on the good stuff too? Tell your employees to start taking ownership of their performance, and the documentation too!

#7: Using Archaic Forms

If so many executives and manager loathe the review, why then do they insist on feeding an already broken process with dated forms? I know it's easy to simply bring forms over from a previous organization or continue to use the outdated ones, but do they really work? Plus, if performance management involves feedback and coaching, are we sure THAT'S even being done? Quit being lazy and put some time and effort into this!

#6: Using an Overly-Complicated Web-Based System

Of course the remedy to archaic forms is an online tool. This takes the manual processing out of the mix. In theory, managers and employees can stay up to date on documentation by simply logging into a web-based tool.

But will they? And if the tool is overly complicated, will the learning curve cause people to ignore it? There are plenty of these tools on the market but most are expensive and hard to use. Not only that, customizing them to your organization can be cumbersome too. If you're going to use on, I'd recommend getting something simple (like my *ProTrack*™ *PMS*) and push people to actually use it!

#5: Using Performance Management as A Way of Getting Rid of Deadwood

Some organizations make it difficult to get rid of poor performers. It can take a manager 18 months to fire a poor performer in the Federal GS system. And that's with good, consistent documentation. If that's the case in your organization, you might be tempted to simply use the annual appraisal to document poor performance since you know you're going to be stuck with employee forever anyway.

But why use this development tool (considering it's probably done annually in your organization) to rid yourself of deadwood when you can simply have the tough conversations and do the documentation now? Poor performers are costing your organization time, energy, and money. Even if it takes 18 months, get busy and make it your mission to fire them! Do everyone a favor and grow a spine! Get busy documenting and firing now. Quit relying on the appraisal to do it for you.

#4: Using a 5-Point Rating System (and Demonstrating It Using the Bell Curve)

5-Point Rating Systems are the obligatory part of appraisals that everyone hates. They allow managers to identify the worth of the employee in a scale that identifies a superstar

(5) and deadwood (1) with gradients in between. In essence, it means we can assign a number to someone that summarizes their value to the organization.

If that alone seems flawed, now lay it against the dreaded bell-curve (you know the one that says only 10% can be superstars and only 10% can be deadwood?) and use that to explain how you rate people. Oh yes, then put in a forced distribution system into the mix (see mistake #2). It's a recipe for accusations of favoritism and general hate and discontent. Ditch the 5-Point Rating System and replace it with frequent conversations where performance is measured real-time.

There is a bonus suck-point: When managers note in the appraisal narrative: *"Sally would have been one of my '5s' but was not due to forced distribution."* Your answer is NOT to continue to over-inflate an already inflated system.

#3: Tying Compensation to Performance Appraisals

I know traditional practice says to tie bonuses and raises to appraisals. After all, how else could you reward good performance? The problem comes when you use an already subjective system to mess with the one thing that causes employees to freak out: their pay!

If you choose to give bonuses, base them on SMART goals and only give them out when the performance makes enough of an impact to generate the kind of cash that would be bonus-worthy. If this doesn't account for cost of living, then simply give a cost of living raise that you already budgeted for.

#2: Implementing a Forced-Distribution Process

If you want to break the morale of your workforce, increase fear and suspicion, and eliminate any sort of trust, have a group of managers meet behind closed doors and "rack and stack" employees into the dreaded bell curve.

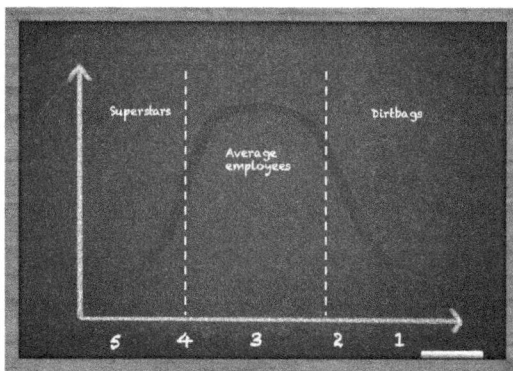

Originally, the idea of bell curved performance was a guide to show managers in a typical organization would have a certain expectation of performance where the majority would fall in between superstars and dirtbags. Unfortunately, CEOs and manager took this a bit too literally and then of course, when you have limited budget to pay bonuses based on performance, you can't have everyone be a superstar or you won't have enough cash for the bonus. So to remedy this, subjectivity is tossed into the mix and employees are forced to wait their turn to be picked as the superstar. Soon they quit trusting the manager, the organization, and their fellow employees. They become hyper-competitive, play less as a team (since there is no direct reward for teamwork), and may even stoop to sabotaging other employees. All so you can have your neat little 5-Point Rating Scale!

#1: Making Performance Management a Once-A-Year Event

Maybe this is what we meant in Point #10. If the annual appraisal is the only time managers talk about performance with employees, there's no guarantee any real results are getting done throughout the year. A once-a-year meeting doesn't have enough energy to make it over 365 days nor should you wait this long to identify and address poor performance. So now that I've shot down most every system done for performance management, what can you do to fix it?

What does it take to do performance management the right way?

It takes a willingness to think of performance

management as a day-to-day process, not a once-a-year appraisal. It involves a commitment from the executive level, not just HR to embrace the process, model the process, and hold managers accountable to work the process.

I know performance management can be difficult and I didn't make your life easier by identifying some of the problems you're already having. I want you to see what the flaws are so you talk intelligently about them when meeting with your executive team. Even if you eliminate a few of the flaws, you can open up better opportunities to implement good performance management practice.

This book is all about winning. When performance management works, everyone wins. Employees work in a productive, focused manner. Managers operate in a less-hectic environment. Corporate objectives are achieved. Profits go up.

That, my friend, is a WIN!

Winning takes work. Read my book and follow the game plan to start the wins with your performance management initiative.

Chapter 1 – All About Performance

Take a look at the diagram below. It's kind of a calendar but it also looks like a clock.

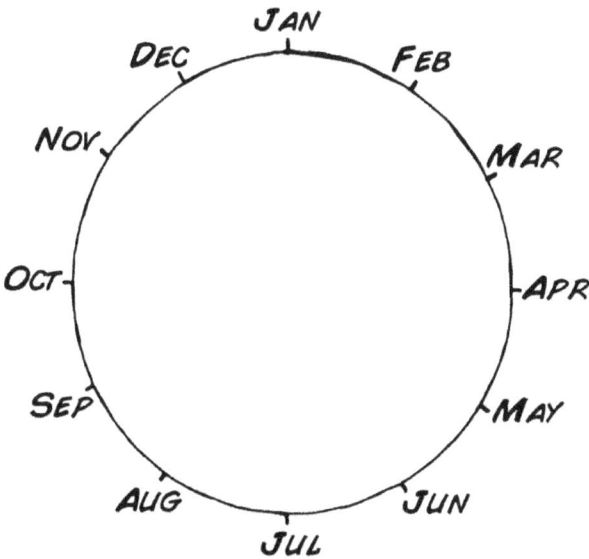

This diagram represents one year. It starts in January and ends in December.

If you were a ten-year old boy, at what point in the year would you need to be on your best behavior?

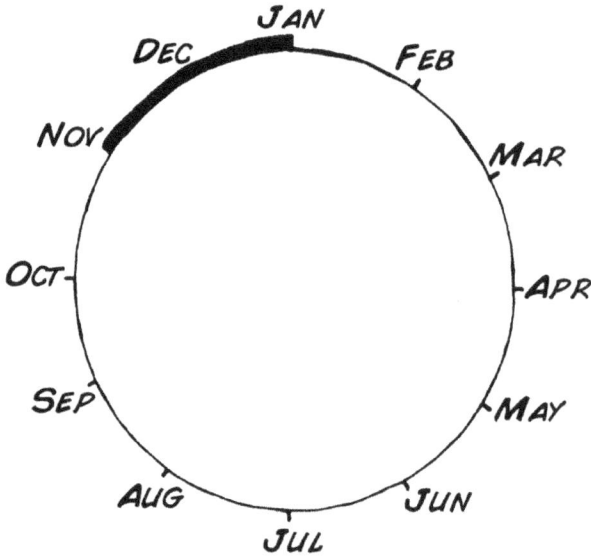

Absolutely! Just a few weeks in November and all of December. I don't care whether you celebrate Christmas, Hanukkah, or Kwanzaa. There is some sort of gift giving that takes place that last week of December.

Now, if we continue with our example using Christmas as our framework, at what time of the year would a ten-year-old boy need to be on his best behavior *IF* he believed in Santa Claus?

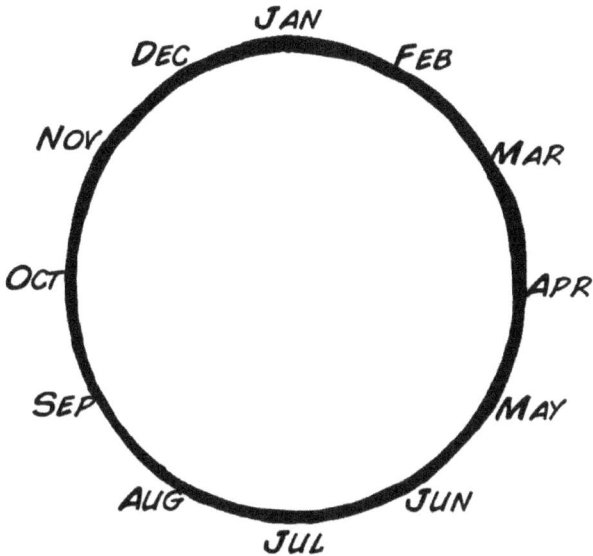

Absolutely! Year round. After all, doesn't Santa Claus know when you're sleeping, awake, blah, blah, blah?

If both boys wind up with the same gift, do you think the second boy will behave well all year long next year? No way! I wouldn't.

What does this have to do with performance management? Everything! Performance management is a daily event, punctuated by periodic evaluation. Done correctly, it results in great performance and strong engagement. People will see a reward for achieving objectives and feel more wedded to the process. Done poorly, it results in jealousy, apathy, and genuinely crappy performance. I know lots of adults that know how to turn on good performance just before appraisal time. I used to do it when I was in the Navy! That's why I'm including a significant amount of information on performance management in a book about engagement. It's a big part of it. It's the longest chapter in my book. That's a clue about how important it is.

Now, when I was a ten-year-old boy, I got a really cool toy for Christmas that year...*the Hot Wheels Power House*. Now if you're not familiar with *Hot Wheels*, they're these little metal cars that you either push around on the floor or run on some specially designed orange tracks made of flexible plastic. The tracks stick together through the use of some plastic purple "tongues" and may even include some curved pieces too. Some of you might have been spanked with one of those orange tracks. I know I was...

The *Power House* however was even more cool. It was a plastic box that sat on the track and contained little wheels inside that spun around when you plugged it into the wall. You stuck your car into the box and the *Power House* shot it around the track. It kind of looked like the diagram on the next page minus the months of the year of course.

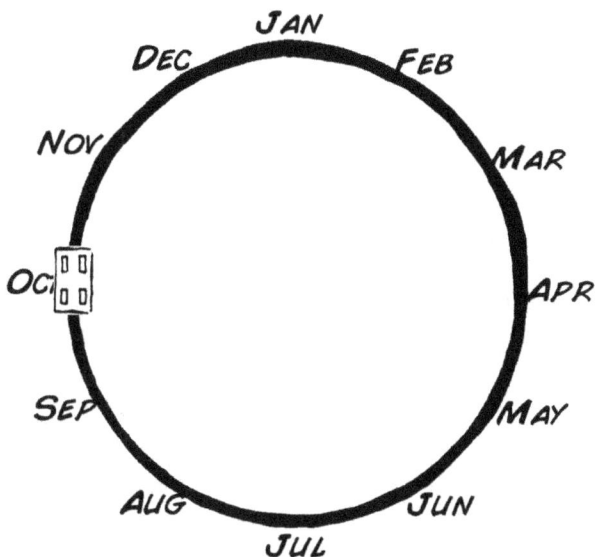

The car would go flying around the track and then slow down just before hitting the *Power House* for another shot of speed. It's kind of like what happens during a performance management cycle that's punctuated by a once-a-year appraisal. You kind of limp in for a shot of motivation.

That same year, my ten-year-old neighbor Larry Rose got a *Power House* too (his was one of his Hanukkah gifts). He brought his over to my house and we rigged up the tracks for maximum power. Now the cars were flying around the track getting a push of power on each turn. That kept us busy for a while, and then we got bored and flipped his *Power House* around so that the cars could crash into each other full force. That's just what ten-year-old boys do.

Can you imagine what kind of performance you could get if you actually checked in multiple times throughout the year with your employees? Look at the diagram.

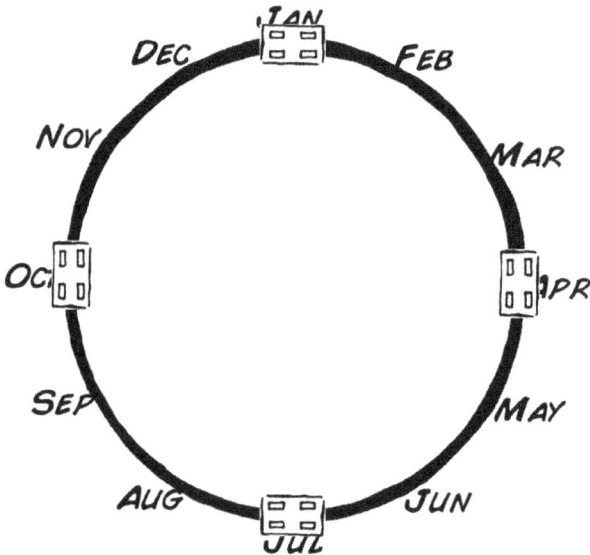

Notice that we're not talking about a formal appraisal here. The appraisal is just a tool.

Real performance management is done on a frequent basis.

Now take a look at the diagram one last time. Notice what happens at each Power House meeting:

Feedback

Feedback is the act of looking back over the previous months and giving an honest assessment. Talk about what you liked and didn't like. Let that employee know in no uncertain terms what you NEVER want to see again and be clear about what you LOVED. By the way, don't wait for this meeting to correct poor performance. Do it when you see it. We'll take a deeper look at feedback later in this book.

Coaching

Coaching is the act of projecting forward what needs to be done in the coming months and giving some assistance. You can do this coaching yourself of find someone who may be good, relevant coach.

Sound simple enough? It really is! People need to have direction and someone along the way to keep them on task and focused on the outcome. This is the most basic and probably most important management skill. I would offer that if you chose to do just one thing as a manager, let it be performance management. If people know that what they do has an impact and really matters to you, they'll feel like they're more a part of the team and thus, more engaged. You'll read a lot more about coaching later in this book.

How do you know what to give feedback and coaching on? Let's first define what makes up good performance. To do that, take a look at the next page at the *Three-Legged Stool of Great Performance*™.

In my workshops, I often ask this simple question:

"How do you know when you're doing a good job at work?"

The answers are predictable.

- *My boss tells me* (followed by a sarcastic smirk).
- *I can just feel it.*
- *I feel good about myself.*
- *Others tell me.*

Then I ask the next question:

"When you're not doing a great job, how do you fix that?"

Blank stares.

Then I show them the following model:

Great Performance

SKILL   **WILL**   **FOCUS**

In a "three-legged stool" model, all legs need to be in balance. Kick one out and you fall on your ass. Have one shorter than the other and you look like a dummy sitting there. All need to be in balance.

The three legs here are **Skill**, **Will**, and **Focus**. Each represents a component of performance that needs to be in balance and each one also has a different impact and remedy to fix it.

Skill

Rob, a Naval Officer, was given a plush assignment as a department head in a large federal agency. It wasn't that he had to apply for the job, it was simply that someone was needed there and he fit the bill.

Rob wasn't quite sure where to begin but fortunately he had an assistant department head that had been there for a while and was well versed in every aspect of the job. Unfortunately for her, Rob never chose to learn how to get the job done. He relied on her and even in meetings was not able to communicate effectively with the group, instead deferring to her each time he was asked a difficult question. While he was successful enough that he was never fired, he never really fully became the department head that that agency needed. Rob could have benefitted from some basic training in the functions of that job.

Skills are the basic basics of doing a job. They can be technical or analytical. When the Skill leg is cracking, the best fix is training. Training can fall in any format so long as it's practical and fixes the issue. Sometimes organizations develop huge training initiatives when really a simple one-on-one can fix the skill issue in question.

But never forget, the only remedy for a skill problem is training.

Will

The Will leg becomes problematic when there are adequate skills but the person simply doesn't want to use them. We often call this an "attitude problem" and the fix is usually some kind of progressive discipline. Sometimes people use training as a fix. Don't be one of them.

A colleague of mine teaches a workshop on communicating with tact and diplomacy. He tells me the class is a tough one since most attendees get SENT to the class. Half of the class typically checks out and sits in the back playing with their smart phones. The other half are bound and determined to make his experience a living hell.

Do you think the attendees KNOW how to communicate with tact and diplomacy? Of course they do! All of us learn at an early age not to tell people they're ugly or fat. They simply choose not to do it. The answer isn't training. It's an expensive mistake to make. Don't do it. Make sure you deal with Will problems appropriately. We will talk at length about dealing with Will in Chapter 2.

Focus

In the classic 1980s movie *The Untouchables*, Elliot Ness, portrayed by Kevin Costner can't make any progress in his battle against notorious gangster Al Capone. It's not until aging beat cop Jimmy Malone, played by Sean Connery agrees to show him the "Chicago Way" in dealing with Capone does he make progress. Malone helps guide Ness's Skill and Will and allows him to be successful.

The Focus leg normally falters when you have a good balance of Skill and Will. Without focus, a driven individual is like a top fuel dragster with no steering wheel and no brakes.

Imagine if you took one of your emerging leaders to a meeting with the CEO and they began telling off-color jokes in the room. You'd want to strangle them right? They know what to do and want to do it; they're just not ready for prime time. The Focus leg is often fixed by mentoring. Let them shadow somebody who knows the ropes. We will talk more about Focus in Chapter 3.

Application

The *Three-Legged Stool of Great Performance*™ is a simple tool but rich in application. It's a guide to accurately diagnosing performance problems. It gives you a guide to diagnosing poor performance and some indicators of how to turn it around. You can then fix them quickly and correctly. Skill and Focus are easy to fix, but what about Will? Chapter 3 will clarify the major components of Will and give you guidance on how to diagnose and fix them in yourself and in others.

Chapter 2 – Where There's A Will, There's a Way

There is no bigger problem a manager faces than a skilled employee who doesn't feel like doing the job. This is a will problem.

Will is all about motivation. It's best summarized using the model below:

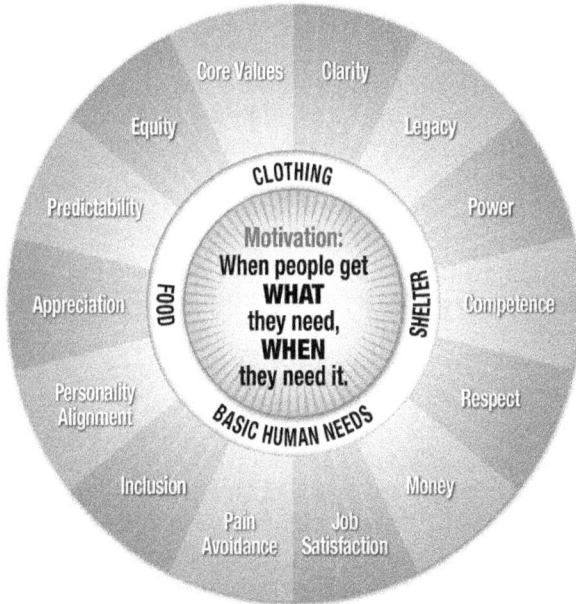

Motivation happens when people get WHAT they need, WHEN they need it. This starts early. An infant can't tell you when they're hungry or need their diaper changed. They cry. When they're taught to use their words then it becomes a bit easier to figure out. As a parent, you're probably used to deciphering moods if you have a pre-teen or dealing with a constant barrage of *"uhdunno"* when you ask your teen why they did something. After awhile you figure it out and then do your best as a parent to give your kids what they need, when they need it.

The model on the previous page differs from some of the motivational theory models you've seen before. Unlike the hierarchies of Abraham Maslow and Clayton Alderfer, and the Two-Factors of Frederick Herzberg, our model starts from the inside and works its way out. Once the basic needs are met, then it's anyone's guess what pops up next. First things first though, the basic needs.

The summer between my son's Junior and Senior years of high school was an exciting time as he prepared for his SAT and did some final college visits. Several events stood between him and graduation, one of which was his student learning hours. He attended a private Catholic high school and they required 40 hours of volunteer time in order to graduate. Knowing that he had a busy schedule and also wanting to keep his part-time job as a cashier at Burger King, he asked us if he could participate in a summer mission trip helping homeless people in Camden, NJ. We didn't have a problem with it even though it meant he (WE) would have to either kick in or raise $600.00. I thought it was a good opportunity for him particularly since he always commented about those "lazy homeless people" who stood in the median strips at our intersections begging for money.

When he returned after his weeklong trip, it looked as though he'd lost about 10 pounds and he's not a fat guy like me! I asked him how his trip was.

"You wouldn't believe this dad," he replied. "They gave us $3.00 per day for food so we could experience what the people we were serving had to live on. You can't buy much for $3.00 so we all pooled our money and bought cans of tuna, day-old bread from the bakery thrift store, peanut butter, and hot sauce since we didn't have enough money for mayonnaise."

Of course my first question was where my $600.00 was spent but then I asked him what he learned.

"It's pretty hard to get motivated to find a job when you're hungry," he said while examining the contents of our pantry. "Wow, we have so much compared to all of them!"

My son learned a life lesson that week that changed his way of thinking... for exactly three days. After that he returned to his normal routine of looking in that same pantry complaining that we had nothing to eat.

He had a point though. When the basic needs are not met, nothing else matters. If you've ever been unable to pay your rent or buy groceries, you know that until that's one, nothing else matters. Today's groups of "doomsday preppers" go to great lengths to build up and protect stores of food and water and build elaborate structures to keep them and their families safe.

I often speak to groups of transitioning military members, usually before they head into the sponsoring job fair. To a person, they all say that no matter what, they just need a job. At that point the need to continue the seamless stream of income they've experienced in their military career is paramount. That's their primary drive.

Ironically though, most former military folks begin looking for a new job within the first six months of their transition. At that point, their income is steady and their initial worry about food, clothing, and shelter is gone. Most of them realize that the job they chose is missing something. Unless they find it, they are guaranteed misery that won't abate so long as they maintain that current job. Military people don't have problems keeping a job; they just have issues expressing what they really want.

They're not alone. If you've ever felt a lack of motivation at work, I'm sure you can understand. There is a lot more to a job, career, or relationship than just money and the basic needs. Unless you know what's missing you won't be able to communicate it in a useful manner. There are many more motivational drivers and each one requires specific remedies solve. They are also unpredictable. You never really know what will pop up when. Motivational drivers are less hierarchy and more *Whack-A-Mole* in nature. If you're a manager, diagnosing them in your direct reports can be a full-time job. Don't fret though; it's the key to figuring out how to get your people busy and productive at work. That's what the remaining markers on my model are all about. Let's start at the top and work our way around.

Clarity

Annie had been working on several important projects in the large manufacturing firm that she had been employed with for the past five years. Recently she became discouraged as members of the executive team stopped many of the initiatives she had been working on. When she asked for clarity she was simply told that many items were still in a state of flux and until that happened no new initiatives would be launched. Frustrated, she began to ask other individuals in the organization if they understood what was going on. At every turn, she was told that nobody really knew. Finally, she told her husband that she was experiencing a severe lack of motivation because everything she worked on was not being moved forward.

"It's almost as if I'm working and yet nobody really appreciates what I do because nobody knows what's supposed to happen," she complained. "I'm not sure how much longer I can put up with this."

Annie's husband told her to hang in there as he was concerned about them losing her salary, but he knew that something needed to be done. He was worried about her, not seeing that same fire that she used to have whenever she talked about work.

What Annie experienced is very common in large organizations. People who are interested in doing a good job need to understand the bigger picture of what they're doing and how it fits in. Organizations that don't have strong communication channels often lose their best performers because seeing how their efforts impact the larger picture motivates them.

If right now you're a manager and are not providing clarity to your direct reports, don't be surprised if their efforts slow down. If you're in a family or a personal relationship and aren't able to clearly communicate goals for either, don't be shocked when your family members or significant other begin to show a lack of motivation. People need to see the destination so they know how to prepare themselves for when they get there. Clarity is a key driver and even if you don't know the answer or have bad news, communicating that alone might go a long way in solving this very important issue.

Legacy

One of my clients engaged me a while back to coach managers who scored low in their annual leadership assessment. In my experience, none of them deliberately set out to score low. In many cases it was a misunderstanding in how the survey instructions were communicated. One benefit of these sessions though was that it gave managers an opportunity to tell me what their motivational drivers were.

One manager who was about 18 months from retirement told me that the most important issue for her was to leave her department in good shape for the person who would replace her. Leaving a positive legacy was a big priority for her.

I experienced this several times while I was in the Navy. I left my assignment on the island of Guam with high spirits and a Navy Commendation Medal. I filled many roles in that two-year tour and felt good about my performance.

About two years later, the old Command Master Chief who I was stationed with in Guam got a transfer to my current command in Washington State. She called me into her office and told me that I "left a huge mess" when I left and my replacement spent months trying to fix what I screwed up.

I was devastated. First of all, I couldn't believe it was true. Secondly though, up to that time I felt great about the legacy I left. My self-esteem plummeted and pretty much sealed my decision to leave the Navy at the end of that enlistment.

A legacy becomes an important driver towards the end of someone's tenure or career. It's a way to properly respect and revere someone's accomplishments. Even if you don't admit it, you want to be remembered in a good way. If you think you're suffering from a lack of this drive, take some time to communicate it with your manager. This is the ultimate in intrinsic motivation and your manager could probably tweak a couple of things and help you finish strong. If you're a manager, make sure you engage your most seasoned employees and ask them how they feel about their legacy.

Power

The summer and fall of 2013 gave us all an example of a dysfunctional government. Regardless of your political leaning, you probably felt a sense of disgust and embarrassment as Congress failed to agree on nearly everything. The Federal workforce experienced a unique indignity as they were furloughed twice, once in the summer as part of the "Sequester" and again in the fall when Congress allowed the Government to shut down.

One of the common refrains I heard living near the DC area was this:

"If Congress was forced to work without pay, they would pass a budget immediately."

I don't buy it. From what I see, people in Congress are already wealthy. They go into government to satiate another need: power. Power is a big driver. It pushed Arnold Schwarzenegger to run for governor of California. It's what causes Donald Trump to make good on his threat a run for President. Money is one motivator, but not as big as power.

Now there's nothing wrong with wanting power. If you feel like a victim at work with no say-so in how things get done, you probably have a need for power. Power is what victims crave to move from victim-stance to a position of control.

If right now you feel like a victim and at a loss for control, money won't provide the long-term solution. Only power can fix it. If you see there's no chance it will happen in your current job, you might face the tough choice of leaving. Don't fret though. It's important to properly communicate what you need; otherwise you won't find a solution.

Competence

Henry was frustrated. He was an experienced mechanical engineer who worked in an aircraft engine manufacturing plant. His new boss Fred Dickerson treated him like an idiot. Fred, whose previous experience was running the finance department, was given this position as he was seen to be on the "fast track" for executive development. He tried to run the manufacturing process like a finance team. He even began requiring Henry to give his progress reports using metrics that made no sense in the engineering field.

Fed up, Henry confronted Fred. He presented his complaints in a logical, unemotional discussion but Fred blew him off.

"Henry," he said, "You may think you know what's going on around here but I'm your manager. We'll do things my way and if you have an issue with it, then maybe you need to transfer someplace else."

Henry was livid. He had a choice to make. Either suck it up and do his job or leave. It was hard for him though. He put his heart and soul into his job and up to this point was seen as the technical expert. Now he had Fred going behind his back trying to short-circuit anything he was working on. Worst of all, Fred had no clue about the engineering field. Henry couldn't believe someone so incompetent had such control over his success.

Henry's experience isn't limited to engineers. Any time you are forced to take orders from someone you think is less competent than you, it's an issue. This is particularly common with personality types that revere competence. The hardest thing for them is to have a reporting relationship with and take orders from a manager who is, in their mind, clueless.

If you're a manager and you have to work with highly skilled, technical people, the best thing you can do is not insult their intelligence. Take the time to learn as much as you can but when possible, defer to their expertise while giving them your perspective so they can see your big picture view. Ironically, the smarter your people feel, the smarter you will look.

Respect

If you're a sports fan, you've no doubt seen this in a post-game locker room celebration. With champagne spraying and whoops and hollers in the background, players are telling their interviewers:

"We're proud to be here. Early in the season nobody gave us any respect but they sure do now!"

Respect means that somebody takes you seriously. In the athletic world, it's usually the team that gets beat early and then is taken too lightly in the championship. At work, it's the person who constantly comes up with great ideas only to have them discounted because they don't have a position of authority. It's the reason why a teen won't listen to their parent but will hear the same suggestion from a friend's parent and will think it's a great idea. Respect means that somebody takes you seriously.

If right now you have a lack of motivation at work or in a relationship, maybe it's the reason. Think of new ways to frame your idea or better yet, have someone in the organization who has respect take your idea propose it, then give you the credit for it. Respect often builds with time and success but if your patience is running out, you might need to think about a new job. Some of my colleagues are seen as thought leaders in the same organizations that years before they were maligned in. When you're part of the organization, you often don't get respect. Coming in later as part of a different company from the outside, it's amazing how much more respect you'll get. Sad but true.

Money

Money is a motivator. No doubt about it. Unless you're independently wealthy, you're working for a paycheck.

I think most people agree though that it's not the sole driver. Many managers think this is what employees want and then fret when they realize there isn't a budget for raises or bonuses.

Don't discount money as a motivator, but don't treat it like the only one. If you can't afford to pay your employees more, remember that there are 13 additional drivers to work with. If you don't feel motivated, don't balk at being turned down for a raise. Money isn't everything, and it's not even the only thing. Keep it in its proper perspective.

Job Satisfaction

People think I'm weird. If you know me, you'd know why. It's not the fact that I collect skulls and have a big beard. It's because I genuinely love what I do for a living. And that means I look forward to Monday and sometimes get depressed when we have a three-day weekend. If that seems sick and twisted to you, then go ahead and keep your current job where you live for the weekend and wish away the workweek. I know some Federal workers who mark their calendars excitedly anticipating "59 Minutes" which is what they often are given off on the Friday before a long weekend.

Most people work to live. I live to work, but I love time with my family. You can do both. Job satisfaction means that you're motivated simply by the job itself and its intrinsic rewards. If you dread Monday mornings, you might be suffering from a lack of job satisfaction. If you don't have a clue of what might give you job satisfaction, be sure to check out my free self-study program *14 Days to Total Career Fulfillment* which you can sign up for using the link in the Appendix.

Pain Avoidance

"I'm motivated because if I don't do the job, I'll be punished."

If that's you, then you represent the second motivational driver most managers espouse. None of us like pain and if pushed, we'll comply to avoid it. As a motivational theory though, it's pretty limited. Once I get through the pain or if I don't fear the potential pain, then I'll simply do what I want to do. Punishment motivates to a point. If you're a manager, use punishment where it's warranted, not as a standard operating procedure. After all, this motivational theory isn't working all that well for Saddam Hussein these days is it?

Inclusion

Carol couldn't wait to begin her first day on the job. She had been actively recruited for month and went through rigorous interviews. Finally, she and got the call she was waiting for and those magic words: *you're hired!*

A month after starting her new job however Carol was depressed. First of all her boss who was so adamant about all the projects he had for her, was nowhere to be found. She didn't have an office to call home for the first two weeks at work, having to share a cubicle with another co-worker. All those hot projects that she had the expertise to fix suddenly didn't have the same urgency that she heard about during her many interviews. Finally none of her co-workers seem to be all that friendly. They looked at her as an outsider, someone to be feared. Carol was not invited to go along for lunch nor was she included in any Friday night happy hours. After 30 more days of feeling like a fifth wheel, she gave her notice and reluctantly returned to her old job.

Inclusion is one of those terms you hear used in that diversity class all of us have had to attend at one time or another. But when we look at it to the lens of motivation, inclusion means that you're feeling like part of the team. If you've ever felt like an outsider or ever had trouble breaking into a new crowd you know the feeling. It probably began when you started a new school and might be something you're experiencing now. Inclusion is a crucial part of organizational introduction. It's one of those things that must to be done shortly after orientation. Onboarding, if done properly, will help make the introductions but it's also important that team members reach out too. If you're a manager, you might want to take extra precautions making sure the new hire feels welcome. If you are new on the job and have yet to feel that sense of being part of the team take some time in contact your manager. Simply being part of an organization on paper doesn't really make a difference if you don't feel like those new co-workers would have your back if you needed them.

Personality Alignment

Willie had a preference for introversion. From the time he was a little boy he always knew that he enjoyed working by himself and didn't like having to do group projects. When he started his new career the first thing he realized was that space in the middle of a large cube farm was not conducive to him doing his best work. All day long he tried to get his projects completed but was continuously plagued by people looking over into his cube asking him stupid questions. Things didn't get much better when he got home either. His wife and kids enjoyed going out and his idea of a great relaxing Friday night was him, a remote control for the TV, and a can of beer. There is nothing wrong with Willie. He just happened to be operating and living in a very extroverted world.

Personality alignment is complicated. If you've ever studied Myers-Briggs or any of those other personality instruments you're probably confused by all the letters and what they really mean. If you get to understand them better though, you know that these personality preferences are some things that we have to live with and don't have much choice in getting in the first place. If you understand your personality, you might have a better idea of why you don't have a sense of motivation. The introversion/extraversion dichotomy is only one of many that can choose to be problematic. If, for example, you are a sensor and have to work with a bunch of intuitives you probably feel as though you're the only one that thinks about the box, not outside of it. If you prefer to make your decisions using emotion, you might feel out of place in a office setting for people use data to make decisions. And if you're one of those kinds of people that enjoys a rigid schedule and a to-do list to track every activity, you might feel like a fish out of water in an office environment where people like to work on last-minute deadlines.

Unfortunately we don't always have a choice on where we work. If you do have a better understanding of your hardwired personality, you can take some steps to pick careers or office settings that are more conducive and if that happens you're very fortunate. At a minimum if you at least understand the way you're wired it might lead to a shared understanding, and if possible some arrangements that might help you even on a temporary basis. Remember, there are no right or wrong personalities, everyone is just different.

Appreciation

Beth had just completed her 25th year as Executive Assistant to the Vice President of Human Resources at a large hospital when she was summoned to the auditorium. When she entered, the filled room stood up and applauded her. Her boss, brought her up on the stage and publically thanked her for her service. The hospital President made a speech. But what brought Beth to tears was the special poem that her co-workers penned that highlighted what they appreciated most: Beth's knack for recognizing special events in the people around her.

For Beth, the act of showing appreciation was recognition enough, but actually recognizing someone who needs it is the best gift of all. If you're intrinsically motivated by your job, then money is nice, but it's that special recognition you get that really motivates. It means that not only do people notice you, they actually value what you do. Showing simple appreciation goes a long way. If you're a manager, take some time to identify those employees who are really motivated by simple acts of appreciation. If you know how to push this button, you'll have the most loyal employee you can imagine.

Predictability

Al was the Director of Logistics for a medium-sized tech firm in Northern California. For the past five years, his team toiled under the command-and-control structure the COO implemented. Al continually fielded complaints from his team and did his best to shield them from the COO's wrath.

Mercifully, that COO suddenly left the company to take a similar position on the East Coast. It happened quickly, with no formal notice. Fully expecting morale to improve, Al couldn't wait to get his team refreshed and productive. Strangely, the team actually showed less motivation. Tension continued and conflict actually increased. Curious as to why, he sought my help.

After doing some digging, here was the issue: Al's team hated the old regime but developed coping skills to deal with it. Now without a common threat, they began to unravel as a team allowing the uncertainty of the new COO's style to keep them in a state of chaos. Strangely enough, having predictable stresses is actually less stressful than having those stresses removed!

Al's team needed some time to vent and to have a formal closure of all the negativity of the old COO's systems and requirements. Without this official transition, predictability was gone and even a bad situation that's known is better than the unknown. Strange I know, but true. If your team can't seem to get back on track after a major change, take some time to dialog with them and put some formal closure on it.

Equity

"That's not fair!"

If you have kids, you've heard this before haven't you? We all want to be treated fairly, even if we can be just a bit more fair than everyone else.

Equity means we feel we're being treated the same as others. Everyone is happy until they find out a new hire makes a bit more money than they do. Suddenly that newbie is lazy and a trouble-maker.

Equity might seem like a childhood driver but it's probably stronger in adults. Whether real or imagined, the perception is something that must be addressed. If you're a manager, make sure you're communicating clearly so there is no chance fairness will come into question. If you're an employee, set up some time to talk with your manager, bringing facts and data to the conversation. If indeed you feel shorted, you need to make your case in a reasonable, data-based manner.

Core Values

Years ago, I was stationed at Naval Dental Center Northwest in Bremerton, WA. My job was to keep the IT systems up and running. Now if you know the Navy, you'll know that each culture has subcultures and the Dental subculture was a classic. It was said (and I believe it's true) that we ate our young. Pity the person who was stationed at a dental facility that wasn't a dental person! Jack was that guy.

He wasn't a star performer. I don't think he really liked his specialty and probably didn't care for the Navy either. The Command didn't like Jack and bounced him around until one day he was assigned to me because supposedly he "liked computers."

When Jack started working with me, I made a conscious effort to see him for what he was, not for what others said about him. He totally amazed me with his dedication and work ethic.

It was him alone that was responsible for the command making massive strides in technology. Sadly, the command continued to shower the credit away from him. Fortunately, he didn't let it bother him and today is a very successful IT professional.

As I think back on those days, I realized that Jack had some core values: things that were important to him. Autonomy, creativity, innovation, and flexibility. All of those were in direct opposition to the Navy which values standard operating procedures and following rules to the letter. Nothing against them. It fits what they do. For Jack it was a drain. The cognitive dissonance he experienced made his life miserable until by sheer accident we found the best fit for him.

If after examining all these motivational drivers you still can't figure it out, then I would challenge you to examine your core values. Do you know what you're about? Do you know what's important to you? What line you won't cross? Then consider the job, company, career, and relationships you have. Are all of them in alignment with you? If not, then something will have to change or you won't ever be happy. Maybe more than any other drive, you need to develop a common language for this one!

So What?

Understanding your motivational drivers is a key part of learning to use your words. If you can't identify what's bothering you, how can you possibly communicate it to your boss? Your spouse? Your neighbors? Your parents? Take some time to carefully reflect on these drivers and develop the dialog you need to have that important conversation.

Chapter 3 – The Focus Factor

While understanding the drivers of motivation can be useful, it's also important to realize there's an "X" factor in this process. We refer to it as the *Focus Factor*.

We know that great performance is a combination of Skill (I know what to do) and Will (I want to do it) but this doesn't explain why some of the most highly skilled and motivated individuals are still unsuccessful at work.

Jaime was a financial analyst at a manufacturing firm in the Northeast. Skilled in his profession and highly motivated, one would have thought he was the perfect employee. Every year at review though, Ed, his manager had a hard time figuring out why he wasn't totally successful. His overall technical performance was stellar, but there was something that was preventing him from being an effective member of the finance team.

If you're a manager, you've probably had the same issues as Ed. In my experience, this is one of the more common problems in employee development. You have people with great skill and great motivation, but there's just something holding them back. If you're not a manager, maybe this is something that you're experiencing personally. You know how to do your job and are motivated to get it done, but there's just something in it that's not a good fit for you.

Seeing a pattern with this, I did my own research and created an assessment called the *MACK Operational Focus Factor Assessment*™ *(MOFFA*™*)* which examines the ideal "focus" areas that a job needs to be done correctly and then an individual component that a worker would take to see if they are a compatible fit for the job. Here's what the model for the tool looks like.

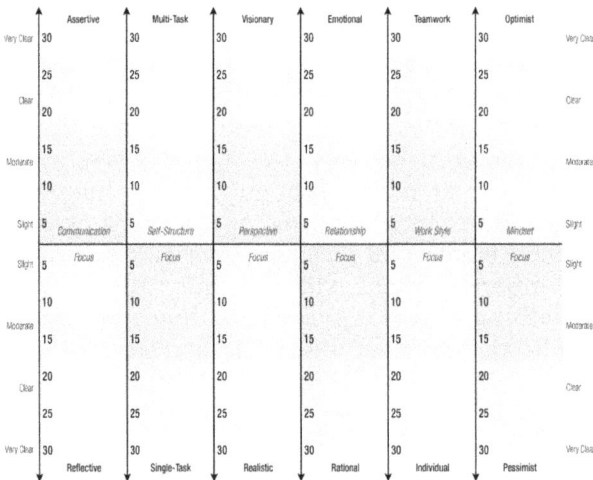

	Assertive	Multi-Task	Visionary	Emotional	Teamwork	Optimist	
Very Clear	30	30	30	30	30	30	Very Clear
	25	25	25	25	25	25	
Clear	20	20	20	20	20	20	Clear
Moderate	15	15	15	15	15	15	Moderate
	10	10	10	10	10	10	
Slight	5	5	5	5	5	5	Slight
	Communication	*Self-Structure*	*Perspective*	*Relationship*	*Work Style*	*Mindset*	
	Focus	*Focus*	*Focus*	*Focus*	*Focus*	*Focus*	
Slight	5	5	5	5	5	5	Slight
	10	10	10	10	10	10	
Moderate	15	15	15	15	15	15	Moderate
Clear	20	20	20	20	20	20	Clear
	25	25	25	25	25	25	
Very Clear	30	30	30	30	30	30	Very Clear
	Reflective	Single-Task	Realistic	Rational	Individual	Pessimist	

The key in using the *MOFFA*™ is taking an honest look at your work requirements. All of us have to make some workplace adjustment to be successful, but our happiness at work tends to be greater when we make minimal shifts. If an employee can be a line for line match, that often leads to a greater level of satisfaction. It's important to realize that there is no "right" style, but there certainly are workplace standards that in fact become the "right" behaviors. Let's take a look at each of the Focus Factors and which industries might have requirements for the accompanying behaviors.

Communication – Our preference in interacting with those around us.

- **Assertive:** Assertive people are comfortable telling you what they want. They tend to take the lead when there is ambiguity and also enjoy working with and around people. Assertive people tend to think out loud and often say things they later regret. Some industries that might value assertiveness might be sales, customer service, law and law enforcement.

- **Reflective:** Reflective people are more comfortable asking for what they want. They tend to sit back and let others lead discussions but are focused on the topic. Reflective people think silently and might come across as slow, but in fact they are processing information at a high rate in their brain. Sometimes they don't speak up and wish later that they had. Some industries that might value reflectiveness might be counseling, health care, the sciences, engineering, and computer fields.

Self-Structure – Our preference in organizing tasks and requirements.

- **Multi-Task:** People who multi-task are comfortable doing many things at once. They look at activity as the best gauge of accomplishment and have difficulty if they are asked to take a task completely from start to finish. Some industries that might value multi-taskers might be air traffic control, food service, nursing, and customer service.

- **Single-Task:** Single-taskers are at their best when they need to focus on just one issue, job, or problem at a time. Their gauge of accomplishment is the finished product. Their gift is to run through a process fully before starting something else. They are hard to distract and if they are, it frustrates them. Industries that might value single-taskers might be the sciences, software developers, engineers, and medical specialties.

Perspective – Our preference in how we see the world and our perspective of it.

- **Visionary:** Visionaries see the future and the possibilities in it. Their perspective is only partially of the here-and-now, and rarely to the past. Visionaries are creative and often find new solutions to chronic problems. Industries that might value visionaries would be R&D, design, and marketing.

- **Realistic:** Realistics see the present and have a clear window to the past. Their perspective is in the here-and-now and seeks visual or concrete proof if they are to believe it. Their gift is the ability to be pragmatic and work within the means or resources at hand to solve a problem. Industries that might value realistics would be accounting and finance, auditing, law, and anything requiring strong implementation skills.

Relationship – Our preference in how we make decisions that impact the people around us.

- **Emotional:** Emotionals use people and people's feelings as a strong basis for making decisions. A good decision will not only solve the problem, but will also take into account the impact it has on the people affected. Empathy is a hallmark of emotionals and they are extremely good listeners and individual problem solvers. Industries that would value emotionals might be nursing, counseling, the clergy, and teaching.

- **Rational:** Rationals use truth, data, and logic as the basis for making decisions. For them, a good decision is fair and objective. It values results over feelings. Rationals aren't completely comfortable with empathy and may find it uncomfortable to open up or to ask others to do so. Industries that might value rationals are the military, law enforcement, first responders, physicians, engineering, and the sciences.

Work Style – Our preference in the work environment that brings out our best performance.

- **Team:** People who prefer the team environment tend to become energized by the interaction and sharing of ideas. A perfect scenario for them would be a group of individual contributors who would share common goals and work synergistically to accomplish them. The camaraderie and communication between the members of the team is almost as important as actually accomplishing the goals. Industries that might value teams are marketing, some manufacturing, elementary and secondary education, first responders, and the military.

- **Individual:** People who prefer individual effort do their best work when they alone are responsible for the outcome. Although completely able to work as part of a team, their preference is to work unencumbered by the needs and complexities of functioning in that environment. The experience of completing a task individually, from start to finish, is almost as important as accomplishing the goals. Industries that might value individuals are sales, medicine, law, consulting, and higher education.

Mindset – Our preference in the outlook we have towards people and events in our lives.

- **Optimist:** Optimists look for the positive in most everything. In demeanor, they come across as friendly and persuasive. They are affective in leading group discussions and brainstorming sessions. Industries the might value optimism are sales, customer service, counseling, and medical.

- **Pessimist:** Pessimists look for truth that can be verified. If not, they tend to disbelieve or disagree with it. Pessimists are often maligned for this character if it's not understood. If maximized, it causes them to often be excluded from discussions and decision-making sessions. Industries that might value pessimism would be engineering, quality control, troubleshooting, and problem solving.

Focus Factors in Action

I sat down with Ed and using the tool, we evaluated Jaime's performance in a new light. Here was the *MOFFA*™ graph for the Financial Analyst position:

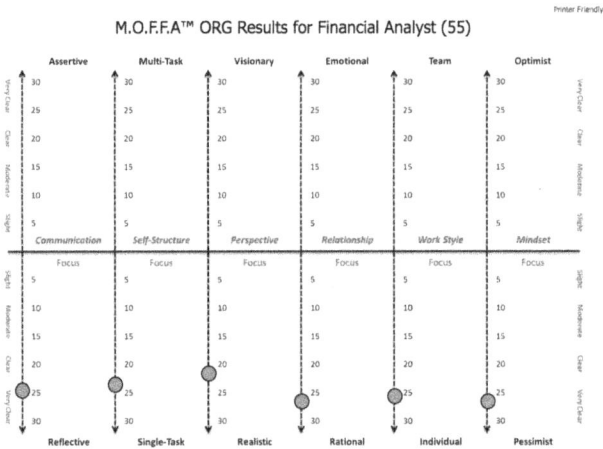

M.O.F.F.A™ ORG Results for Financial Analyst (55)

Notice that the ideal Focus Factors for this position are represented by the grey dots.

Now we had Jaime do the assessment for his work style on this job. His results are plotted in the smaller dots.

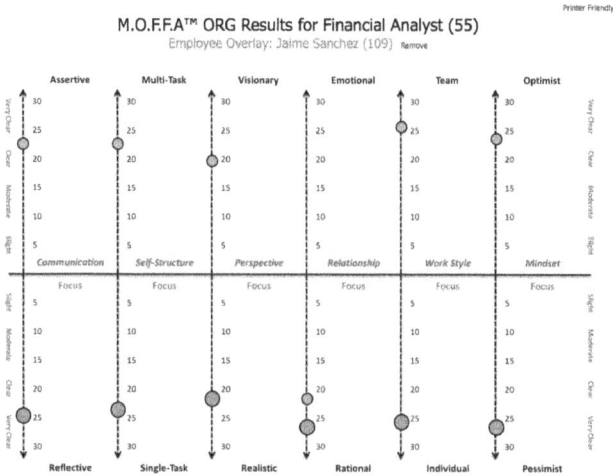

M.O.F.F.A™ ORG Results for Financial Analyst (55)
Employee Overlay: Jaime Sanchez (109) Remove

Looking at Jaime in this lens, we saw that while he was a great and talented worker, his "style" or Focus Factors were a mismatch for the position except for the *Relationship* category. There was nothing wrong with Jaime. He just wasn't a good fit for the job. After sitting down with Ed and seeing the graph, Jaime agreed that he was unhappy in his position even though he was good at his job. With Ed's coaching and guidance, he eventually found a better position within the finance department that was more comfortable for him and let his do his best work.

Can You Fix Focus Problems?

Yes and no. In most cases, a company won't shift focus just to make an employee comfortable. It would be nice but usually not a good idea. Since many of the focus patterns come from "hard-wired" behaviors, there's not much chance of an employee changing their Focus Factors either. In some cases employees might benefit from a coach, but to be effective, the Will must be there.

For you personally, is your current job a good focus "fit" or are you really struggling hard to make it work? Keep in mind that most companies won't adjust for you. It might be time to have an honest conversation with yourself...and then your boss to see if you should move on.

Finally

We've seen so far that Great Performance is a combination of Skill, Will, and Focus and there are clear indicators of success or failure in each. There is one more are we need to explore. In Chapter 4, we'll take a look at development "rounds" and see how that impacts your Will as well as your Skill and Focus.

Chapter 4 – Get In the Ring

While understanding the drivers of motivation and the Focus Factors can be useful, it's also important to realize that circumstance, namely somebody's individual development on a task, can impact the level of Will they might show. In our experience we find there are five levels of development, and each of these levels give us a variety of readings when it comes to those three-legged stool areas of Skill, Will and Focus. Take a look at the model:

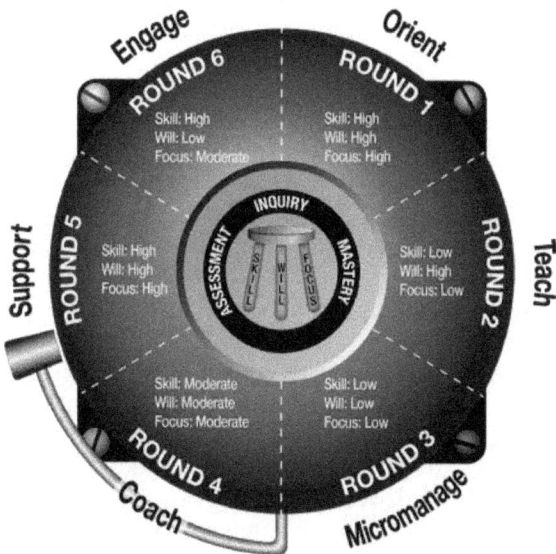

We'll take a look at each "Round" and hopefully what you'll find is the place where you are now or might have been, and understand the common language you need to use to communicate your zone to either your boss, your family, or even yourself.

Basics of the Model

The first area to look at is the inner ring. This is for the individuals who are going through any sort of change process, personal or organizational. The requirement is for them to AIM, which means Assess (taking a look at your own performance), Inquire (figure out what you need to succeed), and then Master (be successful). Then you need to look at the zones themselves. Each one represents a stage of development. Secondly, look at the varying levels of Skill, Will, and Focus. Finally, look on the outside ring at the level of coaching, guiding, and feedback you need from someone to get you to the next zone. That's really the most important aspect here: how to keep moving through the rounds.

Rounds 1 and 2

When my son was 15-and-a-half, he couldn't wait to get his learners permit. I admit we cheated a bit and let him drive a lot during the evenings, but the permit would make it official and legal. We drove to the MVA up in Frederick, Maryland and he easily passed the online test. When we got to the car he couldn't wait and immediately took us home on the interstate. Up to that point we could never get him out of his room, but now he looked for any excuse to drive. The goal of course was to get experience so he could pass his driving test, which he would be eligible for in about six months.

Rounds 1and 2 are all about enthusiasm. It's that first few days on the job where the excitement actually begins when you get the initial offer. It's in the early days of a new relationship where everything is exciting and new. And for most of us it's when we get the opportunity to take on a new challenge. The enthusiasm and high Will is really what sets this zone apart.

The danger is of course that you don't really know yet what you're getting into and you can't seem to focus because you don't know the bigger picture. Still, it's a great time to be alive.

What do you need?

The best thing you can give a person in Rounds 1 and 2 are orientation and some careful guidance. They will come in initially being somewhat overconfident. Because they don't know what they don't know, the best thing you can offer is maybe something like this:

"Here are the first five things you need to do in order to be successful."

It's important to leverage the enthusiasm with training so that the person will be able to navigate the inevitable Round 3.

Round 3

My son had been driving on his permit for about a month when I noticed that he seemed to be a little over confident. He enjoyed driving in my Mazda Miata, particularly when he saw his friends, but I've got a little worried.

One Friday afternoon my wife called to tell me that he had gotten into a minor fender bender. I drove over to the scene, which wasn't far from the house and noticed that he had tagged the side of another driver's car. He was scared and embarrassed. From that point on we noticed that he wasn't interested in driving quite as much. It wasn't as fun as it used to be, and now he realized that there was a lot of things to worry about when he got behind the wheel.

Round 3 is the inevitable, uncomfortable, sure-to-happen outcome after the initial newness of Rounds 1 and 2 wears off. In my son's case it was the realization the driving was dangerous. Maybe for you it's the day you realize that dream job had quite a few flaws and wasn't exactly what you thought you signed on for. It's the day in that new relationship where you suddenly realize that new partner has some serious issues.

What do you need?

While Round 3 is inevitable, it's important to understand there is a way out, but you need to enlist the help of others. On the model this is noted as micromanagement, which nobody ever asked for but when it's needed, it's the best thing you can have.

Your 3-month-old baby is up in the middle of the night screaming their lungs out. You've tried everything to calm them down, from singing, walking around, taking them for a drive the car, and nothing seems to work. In a moment of desperation, you call your mother-in-law and describe your predicament. She tells you to do three simple steps exactly how she says, in the exact order she tells you, and low and behold your baby falls to sleep instantly.

You just got micro managed by your mother-in-law and you loved it! Of course, fast-forward 15 years when she tells you that you're screwing up your kid's life by doing what you're doing, and you want no part of it. When you're Round 3, the best thing someone can do is to take the wheel and steer you out of the ditch and back on the road. I know it sounds counter-intuitive but if you've ever experienced Round 3, and if you haven't I guarantee you will, you will beg for micromanagement.

Round 4

After a few months, my son began to get his confidence back behind the wheel. I didn't see him getting cocky, but rather he would ask us what he should do in certain situations, either behind the wheel, or if maybe his car was broke down on the side of the road. Our goal was to make him independent so that he could make decisions on his own. We were very careful not to spoon-feed him the answers.

What do you need?

Round 4 is that middle ground between complete confidence and moments of incompetence. During this time, you're probably feeling a little bit better but still unsure and terrified of making mistakes. The best thing you could have in Round 4 is someone you can bounce ideas off of. The worst thing you can do at this point is to continually take the person and treat them as though they're in Round 3.

Even though Round 3 is miserable, there is some comfort in knowing that someone will always be there to bail you out. The downside of course is you'll never feel confident to do it on your own. Gentle guidance is the key, meaning you need to find someone you can trust, who you can run ideas by. The goal of course in Round 4 is to get to Round 5.

Round 5

Round 5 is what we refer to as mastery level. Here you are an expert, and nothing will throw you. Your Skill, Will, and Focus are high and you rarely come across something that you don't understand. People come to you with difficult problems and you provide them with solutions.

What do you need?

Round 5 is the goal of everyone, I would imagine: where you are the master of something. In Round 5 you need to have full autonomy, meaning you have what you need to make the decisions that you must make, in order to be successful. The worst thing you can do to somebody in Round 5 is to treat them as though they're Round 3 which means you never micromanage them. If you cringe at that term micromanagement, there's a good bet somebody tried to do it to you when you were in Round 5 and didn't need it. The scary part about Round 5 is that for most people it represents their very best days.

Jim noticed that his boss Kathy always seemed to get in his business. He didn't understand why, but he knew that at one point she had his job and then was promoted to management. What Jim couldn't possibly know was that Kathy was in Round 3 as a manager. She didn't know what she was doing and she didn't know how to ask for help. The only way she could help her confidence get better with to go back to those activities where she knew she was in control. The sad news for her was that nobody recognized this and thus she was stuck in Round 3 for a very long time. Unfortunately for Jim he had to tolerate having somebody get into his business and try to do his job for him while what he needed a strong manager to help pave the way so he could be successful.

Maybe this is the biggest danger of Round 3. If you don't understand it and don't have that common language, you can't possibly get help. Knowing the levels and what they're called so that you can properly communicate what's wrong with you is important.

Round 6

Christy was an expert. People came to her with complicated problems and she always had the solution. It took a while for her to get to this level, but now that she was there, she had a strange feeling that maybe she was burning out. In a way, she missed what it was like learning new things to solve new problems. Now everyday seems about the same and there was no real challenge. She found herself putting less effort into projects and looking for excuses to leave early and not take on any new responsibilities.

What do you need?

Christy is experiencing Round 6. Round 6 is the culmination of a cycle, when you have accomplished great things but it some point realize that there is nowhere else to go. Complacency begins to set in and with it a sense of depression and significant lack of motivation. If you're lucky enough you will have somebody in your life that can come alongside you and ask you honestly what's going on. Round 6 requires caring inquiry so you can understand where you're at.

If you're struggling in Round 6 what you need most is a new challenge, something that will be a little out of your comfort level and gives you something to strive for. The interesting thing is that when you look at it, you find that it's usually a task that is Round 1 and 2 in nature. You'll get excited, looking forward to new challenge. Your Skill, and Focus will probably be low, but your Will be high. If you follow the model, you know that you're just making another lap around the track. You'll go to Round 3 as sure as the sun comes up in the morning. It'll be a struggle and then of course comes Rounds 4 and 5. After a period of time, you'll go back to that Round 6 experience, seeking new challenges.

The beauty of the process is that the more we go around the track the stronger we become the more valuable we are to ourselves, our families, and our organizations. Human beings are wired to grow and if you understand the way development happens, you'll seek out what you need when you need it to get you through each of the development Rounds.

Chapter 5 – Feedback

Feedback is a look at the individual's past performance. It involves evaluating results and making comments on what was good and also what was bad. It's the manager's opportunity to assess where areas of growth might be. This is your first set of skills you'll be using when helping that employee navigate the development rounds.

When giving feedback, it's important to pay attention to the following:

1. **Focus on behaviors, not the person.**
   - Describe them as you saw them; put your observation in the "I" form.
   - Describe the impacts the behaviors are having on you and the other employees.

2. **Be specific.**
   - Use examples as often as you can.
   - Point out the particulars of the behaviors.

3. **Be realistic and sincere.**
   - Focus on those behaviors that the employee can change.
   - Describe the value of making the change.
   - Describe your feelings and the impacts on the rest of the team.

4. Say it when you see it.
- Provide your feedback as close to the behavior as possible.
- Positive feedback reinforces positive behavior; negative feedback diminishes negative behavior.

5. Do it frequently.
- Frequent feedback is more effective than periodic feedback.
- Frequent feedback allows you to create a theme, or your teaching points.

6. Make yourself clear.
- Let the employee know why you are providing the feedback.
- Summarize the priority points of your feedback.

Watch Out!

While no manager would intentionally be biased towards certain employees, it still happens. Here are some of the most common biases and what they can result in.

Halo effect. This happens when a person is good at one skill or task and the supervisor considers them to be good at everything they do. The Halo effect leads to higher, but less accurate assessment ratings

Horns effect. This is the opposite of halo, and happens when a person is bad at a skill or task and the supervisor rates them lower on everything else as well. The Horns effect leads to lower, less accurate ratings.

Central Tendency. Central Tendency happens when a rater does not rate subordinates as being particularly good or bad at anything. Instead, they rate them in the middle ratings, as just OK. Central tendency is an error because everyone has strengths and weaknesses. These strengths and weaknesses should be evident in performance ratings.

Recency Error. This occurs when a supervisor rates performance based only on their most recent behaviors, accomplishments, or failures.

Leniency Error. This occurs when you have a positive overall opinion of an employee, or a particularly close relationship with them. In this case, you may be inclined to give them more favorable performance ratings than what they have actually earned.

Severity Error. This is the opposite of Leniency and happens when you have a poor opinion or a bad relationship with an employee. As a result, you might give them less favorable ratings than what their performance has earned.

Similar-to-Me Error. This occurs when your view of the employee is that they are like you. In this case, you may give them more favorable ratings.

Different-from-Me Error. This is the opposite of Similar-to-Me and results in lower ratings.

Spillover Error. The Spillover Error is when you give ratings based on your opinion or assessment of the employee's performance in past performance periods. For example, an employee may have had poor or mediocre performance for the past couple of years. Their performance has improved this year, but your ongoing opinion of them is that they are a poor performer. As a result, you give them lower ratings.

Status Error. The Status Error occurs when you are rating an employee that has a particularly good social or political position in the department or company. This is more likely to occur if you are rating a peer or supervisor, but can also occur when rating employees. In this case, you may be hesitant to give the employee lower ratings than what their performance warrants.

Since giving feedback can be uncomfortable, it's a good idea to prepare beforehand by using a script. While you wouldn't simply read the finished script to the employee, it is a way to get your thoughts in order. Here are two that I find useful:

The Standard Script

The Standard Script works for most instances of poor performance and also for good performance.

When I observed you doing or saying... (Be specific.)

It made me feel... (the impact it had on you.)

It also affected the team and what we are trying to do... (the impact it had on everyone else).

What do you think about what I just said?

...Pause for the employee's response.

I need you to... (the new behavior that you want to see).

How do you feel (or what do you think) about that?

This script makes YOU the owner. You have to take the responsibility so use the "I" statements.

The Red Alert Script

One of my old bosses would use the term "Red Alert" whenever he saw a problem in the clinic I managed. It sort of stuck with me. The

Red Alert script works when you need to correct a bad behavior quickly on the spot.

1. **Objectively state what you have observed.** *("Hey you were an hour late this morning")*

2. **Allow them to respond.** (Let them tell you what happened. Don't let them off until they come up with something. Be patient. Get ready for a bunch of lame excuses.)

3. **Reiterate your expectations.** (Remind them of the policies, expectations, etc.)

4. **Make them own the solution.** (Let them come up with their strategy to fix the problem)

5. **Mutually agree on this solution** (Be sure to document and hold them accountable)

Make sure you do this type of feedback in private. Don't let your emotions affect you, either by being too soft or too harsh. You must get the employee in line and protect yourself and your company.

With feedback done, now it's time to help the employee get better! It's where coaching comes in.

Chapter 6 – Coaching

Coaching, which I also consider to be a form of guiding, is used to help an employee build skill and focus. I use the word "guiding" because "coaching" is an industry with a regulating body designed to prevent hacks from giving bad advice. For the manager in a workplace who is helping an employee get more effective, we mean "guiding" but for the purposes of this book I'll just call it "coaching."

When doing coaching, it's important that you clearly identify the gap in the employee's performance and assist them in filling it. Also, keep in mind that depending on the "round" the coachee is in, your coaching approach will be different. To do that, I recommend the following PUSH/PULL methodology:

PUSH Coaching (Rounds 1, 2, 3 and 6)

- **P: PICK** an issue to deal with
- **U: UNDERSTAND** the current situation
- **S: STRONGLY** suggest solutions
- **H: HOLD** them accountable

PULL Coaching (Rounds 4 and 6)

- **P: PICK** an issue to deal with
- **U: UNDERSTAND** the current situation

- **L: LEARN** more through open-ended questions
  L: LEAD them to a solution

Again, it's important to figure out where the employee is in their development. You can't screw this up! We do that with the P and the U.

Step #1: PICK one issue to address

Step #2: UNDERSTAND the current situation.

Let's say we're talking to Bill about his performance.

You: *"Bill I'd like to talk about to you about your short temper when we do our staff meetings. Can you tell me what's going on?"*

Bill: *"I'm just frustrated. I've been here for six weeks and just can't seem to get the routine down around here. I feel like I'm not grasping things. I almost wish I had never left my last job."*

Bill is clearly fighting Round 3. He needs YOU to bail him out. So you do that by STRONGLY SUGGESTING what he should do and then HOLD him accountable to those suggestions.

Let's look at another scenario. You're talking to Jane about her performance.

You: *"Jane, I'd like to talk to you about your short temper when we do our staff meetings. Can you tell me what's going on?"*

Jane: *"I'm just frustrated. I've been in this role for 3 years now and I think I just need a new challenge."*

Jane is fighting Round 6. It's time to engage her in a conversation about her career goals so we would LEARN more through open-end questions and then LEAD her to a solution. This won't excuse her current behavior but it might just solve the root issue. She is outgrowing her role and needs a new challenge.

PUSH coaching is pretty simple. You've probably done it more times than you know.

PULL coaching on the other hand takes practice. The key is to listen and to ask open-ended questions. You need to learn more so you ask and listen. The following are what I consider to be the "Greatest Hits" of open-ended questions.

Tell me more about that.

This is an invitation for the coachee to open up. They may start off with a statement like "I feel like my career is at a dead-end right now." Your response? "Tell me more about that."

What does that look like?

Listen to the words they use. Every time you hear something that sounds like a metaphor, ask to clarify. Words like *disaster, train wreck,* etc. need to be unpacked. You have to figure out what's going on to elicit that response.

Hmmm, that's interesting.

This is your chance to tell the coachee they're being an idiot, without actually telling them that. Here's an example:

- **You:** "So tell me what's going on."
- **Them:** "I'm frustrated with one of my co-workers."
- **You:** "Tell me more about that."
- **Them:** "I think they must be stupid or something. I try to communicate but they don't seem to respond. I think next time I'm to slap them across the face to get their attention."
- **You:** "Hmmm, that's interesting."

The coachee is obviously frustrated. Your statement lets them know it's not appropriate to react that way, even in jest. But at least you're doing it in a nice way.

And what happened when you tried that?

As the coachee is going through the story with you, they'll share some of their ideas. When they've already tried one or two, ask them what happened when they tried it. Get their honest assessment. Remember when using these questions, the coachee is in either Round 4 or 6 so they have some skills. At a minimum they should have tried some solutions.

How do you feel about that?

This is a great question to ask when you don't know what to ask next. Listen to the answer and then use that as a springboard to the next question. Nobody can argue what a person feels so this is your chance to sit in curiosity, not judgement.

And how is that working for you?

This question is one of TV psychiatrist Dr. Phil's favorites. He uses it when one of his guests are struggling with something and start to get desperate with solutions, or at a minimum have caused much of their own problem.

- **Dr. Phil:** "Tell me what's going on Jim."

- **Jim:** "Well Dr. Phil, I have a wife...and a girlfriend...and a boyfriend."
- **Dr. Phil:** "How's that working for you?"

Dr. Phil wants to let the guy know he's caused some of this stress. Maybe if he owns that, then a resolution can be reached.

Use this one carefully. You're not Dr. Phil.

What would a perfect resolution look like?

When a person is fighting Round 4 and 6, they get discouraged. When they start getting negative, bring them back with this question:

What would a perfect solution look like?

Wait for then answer, then...

What's one thing you could do to make that happen?

Now let them take a little ownership. Get them to come up ideas. Don't let them wallow in the negativity too long.

Can I offer you a suggestion?

This is the transition that can bring in some elements of PUSH coaching, but be careful. Remember, you want to LEAD the coaching to the solution, not feed it to them.

When they want your suggestion, avoid this:

Well if I was you, I'd....

First of all, you are NOT them. Secondly, you want them to own this, not to what YOU would have done. If they fail, they can simply blame you. Instead, try one of the following:

What would happen if...?

Have you ever thought about...?

These two questions make your advice (probably great advice) sound like suggestions. I know it sounds like you're just feeding the answers and you are, but they'll probably implement them since they think it's their idea. They'll own it. That's what you want isn't it?

Finally

Just remember this:

- For **PUSH** coaching, the <u>MORE</u> you say, the SMARTER you look.

- For **PULL** coaching, the <u>LESS</u> you say, the SMARTER you look.

If you want to look like a dummy, simply reverse the rules!

PULL coaching takes practice and as a manager, it's something that YOU can benefit from as well. Find some trusted colleagues and spend a little time each month working each other through the methodology.

Finally, when an employee seems at an impasse due to issues that you can't seem to pin down, consider using resources that your company's EAP might provide. Employees may also benefit from working with a professional, certified coach. This might be a pricy alternative but worth every penny if your employee is a keeper! I recommend getting a coach from Wisdom Tree Coaching which you can find at *WisdomTreeCoaching.com*.

Chapter 7 – Self-Assessments

Performance management isn't just the manager's job. Employees have two key responsibilities:

1. Do the job
2. Document their performance

We expect employees to get the job done. That's what they get paid for. But since we can't be everywhere or see everything, it's important to get employees to take some time to document their performance.

To help employee's better document, it's important we determine the three types of jobs they do and give them an easy tool for documentation.

3 Types of Jobs

The "Heartbeat" Job

Right now you're probably thinking about your heart beating but if it stopped, you'd know. That's kind of like the basic job an employee does. The tasks are described in the job description. If an employee does the job, he gets paid. If he doesn't, he can get fired. Like the heartbeat. If it happens, we function. If it doesn't, we shut down.

There shouldn't be a self-assessment for this type of job. You either do it or you don't if you do it, you get paid. If you don't, you get fired. I don't recommend bonuses for these.

The Objective-Driven Performance

If your organization has strategic objectives, you might have to help an employee develop goals to get it done. Most companies use the SMART format. Writing a goal takes practice and we won't cover it here.

Writing the goal is just the beginning. The employee must accomplish the goal satisfactorily and then document it. If you're helping employees write good goals and they achieve them, there should be a noticeable improvement on the bottom line. If that's true, then you'd better be sure they know how to document. I have a tool for that you'll read about shortly.

The Value-Based Behavior

While the objective-driven performance talks about WHAT the employee does, it's also important to pay attention to HOW they do it. This is where values come in.

Most companies I work with have corporate values. These are the written guidelines such as teamwork, sustainability, integrity, honesty, or any other desired behavior descriptor. You can also throw in any of the Focus Factors from the *MOFFA*™ tool.

These are important. You can have a first-rate salesperson on your team who can close anything but if she undercuts her team to get those commissions, she's not living the value. That needs to count against her.

DOING the work is only part of it. Employees also need to document what they do and why it mattered. This creates accountability and ownership. It also makes your job as a manager a lot easier. To help, I have a couple of tools that you can teach to your employees: OGRE™ and VSCAR™

Follow the next steps and see how OGRE™ and VSCAR™ work.

Goals – What We did to Meet the Objectives
Unit or Department
- Evaluated by evidence of the "M" in S.M.A.R.T.
- Based on results (dollars, numbers, or percent).
- Should be formally evaluated quarterly but employee self-assessment and input should be frequent (weekly or bi-monthly).
- **Either MET or DID NOT MEET.**

Individuals
- Self-Evaluated individually through the use of **O.G.R.E.**
  - **O**=which objective was targeted.

- o **G**=which goal were you working on.
- o **R**=what were the results? (based on the "M" in S.M.A.R.T.).
- o **E**=evaluation – where did you see the link between your action and its accomplishment?
- Should be formally evaluated quarterly but employee self-assessment and input should be frequent (weekly or bi-monthly)
- **Either MET or DID NOT MEET.**

Corporate Values – How We Met Our Objectives (Behaviors)
- Evaluated through a peer recognition ("assists").
- Evaluated individually through the use of **V.S.C.A.R.**
  - o **V**=The value you embraced or demonstrated through your action.
  - o **S**=The situation you faced that pushed you into action.
  - o **C**=The particular challenge you addressed.
  - o **A**=The value-based action you took.
  - o **R**=The overall result of your action.
- **Either EXCEEDED, MET, or DID NOT MEET.**

The "Heartbeat" Job (what we get paid to do)
- Evaluated through observation and based on result, both tangible and expectations.
- Should be evaluated by the manager on a regular basis.
- **Either MET or DID NOT MEET.**

Documentation is key. I recommend both managers and employees take five minutes each week to reflect upon and document accomplishments of that week.

Keeping track of this can be cumbersome but fortunately we've developed a great system called *ProTrack PMS* which enables managers and employees to log into a website to record accomplishments. Then, when you do your quarterly reviews, it's super easy to get all the OGREs™ and VSCARs™. It also enables employees to recognize each other for accomplishments. If you're interested in a demo, contact us at (931) 221-2988.

Performance Management

O.G.R.E.

Chapter 8 – Now What?

The models and processes in this book are designed to help you succeed as a manager. Your key responsibility as a manager is to develop your team. Depending on your company's performance management system is one thing, but the hard work you do each day of giving feedback and coaching will make the difference. Make a commitment today to take this responsibility seriously. Your people and your organization will appreciate it!

GREAT PERFORMANCE

About the Author

Mack Munro is Founder and CEO of **Boss Builders** and is an experienced speaker and consultant, and who has worked with executive and management teams in companies of all types, sizes, and industries in the USA and abroad. He is the author of *How to Be a Great Boss* and three other business books.

He holds a Master of Arts degree in Organizational Leadership from Chapman University and a Bachelor of Science degree in Health Care Management from Southern Illinois University He is a qualified facilitator of the Myers-Briggs Type Indicator® and has also written and developed a number of personality and behavioral assessments and online tools.

Mack's background is primarily in Healthcare, Manufacturing, Consulting, Information Technology, Entrepreneurship, Leadership & Management, and Marketing. His typical clients come from these areas.

Prior to starting his company, Mack created training and professional development programs at U.T. Medical Group, Inc. in Memphis, TN,

Holy Cross Hospital in Silver Spring, MD, and Contract Services Association of America in Arlington, VA. Mack has been an adjunct Professor of Business and Management at Vincennes University in Bremerton, WA and Crichton College in Memphis, TN. He a retired United States Navy dental technician who served tours in Australia, Guam, Long Beach, California, and Bremerton, Washington.

Mack's clients include Pratt & Whitney, UTC Research, Pitney Bowes, Munters Corporation, Connecticut Online Computer Center, Bridgestone, CU Direct, numerous Federal agencies, and all 4 branches of the United States Military. He has delivered keynotes to groups and associations around the country and internationally, and is a regular speaker at the Society for Human Resource Management (SHRM) state and local chapter meetings.

He has been featured as a career expert on radio, television, and printed and electronic media, including a monthly column in *Men's Fitness* magazine.

You can reach Mack for speaking engagements on his blog at:

www.MackMunro.com

Mack Munro
P.O. Box 75
Vanleer, TN 37181
(931) 221-2988
Mack@TheBossBuilders.com

How Boss Builders Partners with You to Build Better Bosses

We have three options available to help you, the busy and stressed HR professional improve the competence and confidence of your company's managers.

Option #1: Our Onsite *Driving Results*® Instructor-Led Workshops

***Driving Results*® Onsite Workshops** are the most efficient way to train a small group of Bosses (between 10 and 30 participants) if you prefer live training at a location of your choosing.

This program, if delivered from start to finish, is four-days long. We can deliver it for you in half or one-day increments if you like.

Benefits:

- Interactive training and the opportunity for live skills practice.

- Opportunity to weave current participant challenges into the workshop.

- No travel expenses for attendees.
  If you're interested in us bringing our training onsite to your organization, we are happy to

oblige. Here is our standard course offering. Scroll to the very bottom for pricing.

Option #2: Our Boss Builder Academy Video Series

Boss Builder Academy is best for organizations that want to train multiple new Bosses.

- Boss Builder Academy kickoff (live or webinar) with a Boss Builder facilitator
- Structured guidelines for coaching and giving feedback to Boss Builder Academy participants by their manager
- Pre and Post Phase online evaluations to measure the growth and learning of the participants
- 12 month subscription to the video content
- Access to the *BossFlix*™ video library
- All worksheets and handouts for the videos and webinars.

Option #3: *Driving Results*® Curriculum License and Purchase

License and Materials

This license gives company the right to purchase and deliver our Driving Results workshops to your team. The license stays with your organization for as long as you like and does NOT transfer to any individual if they leave your company. Former employees can purchase a license in their new organization if they choose. This protects your investment.

The license gives you access to a robust instructor guide which includes a slide-by-slide video demonstration with suggestions on delivery techniques. You'll also have access to any product updates via a dedicated learning portal. A certified Boss Builder facilitator can be onsite to walk you through set-up or co-instruct with your trainers on a per-day basis. This rate is available when you open your quote as an option.

Each attendee must purchase a workbook and assessment which is priced per-user in the quote. These will be marked up in a class as there are many fill-in-the-blank areas.

**For more information on how Boss Builders
can help you develop better Bosses, contact
us at:**

Mack Munro
P.O. Box 75
Vanleer, TN 37181
(931) 221-2988
Mack@TheBossBuilders.com

BOSS BUILDERS

.